BRITAIN IN OLD PHOTOGRAPHS

BLACK COUNTRY
ROAD TRANSPORT

J I M   B O U L T O N

ALAN SUTTON PUBLISHING LIMITED

Alan Sutton Publishing Limited
Phoenix Mill · Far Thrupp · Stroud
Gloucestershire · GL5 2BU

First published 1995

Copyright © Jim Boulton, 1995

Cover photographs: (front) Charabancs on
Wolverhampton Market Place, 1920s; (back)
the legendary George Dance riding his
Sunbeam ohv sprint machine, *c*. 1919.
Title page photograph: The author's first
encounter with motors in 1925 – a 1912
BSA car at his father's garage.

British Library Cataloguing in Publication Data.
A catalogue record for this book is available from
the British Library.

ISBN 0-7509-0852-1

Typeset in 9/10 Sabon.
Typesetting and origination by
Alan Sutton Publishing Limited.
Printed in Great Britain by
Hartnolls, Bodmin, Cornwall.

For Libra's Christine and Judy

THE BLACK COUNTRY SOCIETY

This voluntary society, affiliated to the Civic Trust, was founded in 1967 as a reaction to the trend of the late 1950s and early 1960s to amalgamate everything into large units and in the Midlands to sweep away the area's industrial heritage in the process.

The general aim of the Society is to create interest in the past, present and future of the Black Country, and early on it campaigned for the establishment of an industrial museum. In 1975 the Black Country Museum was started by Dudley Borough Council on 26 acres of totally derelict land adjoining the grounds of Dudley Castle. This has developed into an award-winning museum which attracts over 250,000 visitors annually.

There are over two thousand members of the Black Country Society and all receive the quarterly magazine *The Blackcountryman*, of which over 105 issues have been published since its founding in 1967. In the whole collection there are some 1,500 authoritative articles on all aspects of the Black Country by historians, teachers, researchers, students, subject experts and ordinary folk with an extraordinary story to tell. The whole constitutes a unique resource about the area and is a mine of information for students and researchers who frequently refer to it. Many schools and libraries are subscribers. Three thousand copies of the magazine are printed each quarter. It is non-commercial, and contributors do not receive payment for their articles.

PO Box 71 · Kingswinford · West Midlands DY6 9YN

Contents

'The' BEAN FOURTEEN

A world's record of which Dudley can be proud

WITH a load equivalent to 16 twelve stone passengers, the BEAN Five-Seater Illustrated successfully crossed Australia twice—a total distance of 6,200 miles or almost a quarter of the earth's circumference.

The journey was made to investigate projected railway routes and lay through the trackless bush, over stony deserts and sandy dried-up gullies. Yet in spite of these almost incredible conditions the BEAN won through and is the only car to have crossed Australia, North to South.

Such is the service every BEAN is built to give—for this was a standard model which had already run over 14,000 miles.

Then remember the BEAN is made in Dudley by local workpeople. Buy a BEAN and support local industries.

Dunlop Tyres fitted on all models.

The Twelve from £335.   The Fourteen from £395.

A. HARPER, SONS & BEAN LTD.
Head Office and Works   -   -   -   DUDLEY, Worcs.

Distributors—

WHORTON & CHRISTOPHER
HIGH STREET, DUDLEY.

14 Five-Seater
£395

An advertisement from Blocksidge's *Illustrated Dudley Almanac, Diary and Directory,* 1925.

Introduction

Vehicle manufacturing was an important part of Black Country industry. Every type was produced there including railway locomotives and aircraft. It was said that any part of a motor vehicle could be obtained from the Black Country.

In this book I have collected photographs and details of some of the products of this unique area: cars, local transport and passenger vehicles, and some specially built for competition work. There are also some photographs of vehicles made elsewhere but used by Black Country operators.

From the earliest days there were coach builders in this area, one of whom, Alfred Forder, became famous for Hansom cabs. He also built a few velocipedes (boneshakers) which were raced at Molyneux Grounds in 1869.

The Wolverhampton cycle industry was established in 1869 and by 1871 had over fifty separate makers employing more workers than that industry in Birmingham. Later, from these beginnings, Wolverhampton's motor vehicle manufacturing became very important.

The first mechanically propelled passenger vehicles made in the area were built by the Electric Construction Corporation (later Company) at Bushbury. These were battery powered. One model, a double-decker omnibus, saw service in London during 1891, and several single-deckers followed. Cars were also produced and an 1897 model was a true horseless carriage – for its single front wheel was steered by reins. A petrol car was experimented with in 1897, but the Electric Construction Company decided to concentrate on electrical equipment, for which the company justifiably became world renowned.

The first serious motor manufacturer, Edward Lisle, had from 1869 built up a considerable cycle-making business. By 1896 he was producing about a hundred Star cycles a week. Fearing a decline in sales because of cheap imports he decided to enter the field of automobile manufacture. A German Benz was acquired and in 1899 a Star car based on this model was offered. At first one a week was produced. The business grew, and by 1914 the Star Company was one of the six largest British car manufacturers.

The sons of another pioneer Wolverhampton cycle-maker, Henry Clarke, from 1899, were offering motorcycles under the Wolf and Wearwell trade marks.

John Marston, who owned a successful japanning business, built his first cycles in 1886. In 1888 came the first of his superb Sunbeams. Sometime around 1899 experiments were made with motors, though his first production in this field was the strange licence-built Mabley. Conventional Sunbeams were built in small numbers and in 1905 a separate Sunbeam Motor Car Company was established. In 1909 the great French engineer Louis Coatelen joined the firm, and soon a hundred Sunbeams were being sold each year. The manufacturing works became one of the finest in the industry and the company gained world fame for superb cars and for competition successes. John Marston continued making cycles and, from 1911, motorcycles. The latter also became world famous for quality and international competition success.

One of the first powered two wheelers, certainly the first in the Black Country, was built by the Stevens brothers in 1898, but their main business was making engines for sale to other firms. Fees received for the design of the first Sunbeam motorcycle engine enabled the brothers to achieve their ambition of producing complete machines. During 1910 AJS was born, and the company became the makers of one of the world's great motorcycles. Production reached 600 a week.

The First World War rapidly increased people's experience of mechanical vehicles, and after hostilities many wished to own their own motors. There was a boom in sales and many new companies set up production. The inevitable slump followed in the late 1920s and many of the new companies ceased to exist. The old established manufacturers also suffered.

Dudley ironfounders, Bean, established in 1826, had expanded considerably during the First World War and in 1919 a decision was taken to become part of a consortium with very ambitious plans to challenge Ford Model T production, with 100,000 cars and commercial vehicles *per annum* as a target. This did not materialize, but the Bean car became very popular and was seen as a rival to the Morris with a hundred cars a week being produced. The chassis was made at Tipton and then driven to Waddam's Pool, Dudley, for body fitting. Financial problems brought the closure of the company in 1933, but it rose again as Bean Industries to manufacture components. The company was chosen to build Captain George Eyston's World Land Speed Car of 1937/8, 'Thunderbolt'. The company became part of the Austin Rover Group and later there was a management buyout. During 1994 the company rescued Reliant Motors, a customer for engines that was in financial trouble, but then itself ran into financial difficulties. The company has recently been bought out again but now has a very reduced workforce.

The other Black Country mass producer of cars, Clyno, had moved to Wolverhampton from Northamptonshire, where they had started motorcycle production in 1909. Large numbers of machines were produced, including machine-gun outfits from 1914. From 1922 only cars were made. Peak production was 600 cars a week and for a time Clyno outsold the Morris Cowley.

The 1920s was the golden age of Black Country motor vehicle production with numerous concerns manufacturing cars, motorcycles and commercial vehicles. Most of these were good, some were excellent and had good export markets. Guy Motors, founded in 1914, had large military contracts and built on that foundation in peacetime.

By the 1930s the local vehicle industry was in decline. Price cutting wars brought the Receiver to Clyno in 1929, by which time some 15,000 motorcycles and 40,000 cars had been sold.

AJS also ran into difficulties and was liquidated in 1931. It was taken over by AMC and production moved to their London works. In 1937 AMC also acquired Sunbeam cycle and motorcycle names but did not continue the marque.

Guy Motors had owned Star since 1928 and liquidated it in 1931. The Sunbeam Motor Car Company had financial problems over many years and was acquired by Rootes Securities in 1935. No further Sunbeam cars were produced other than badge engineered products of the Rootes Group. However, the production of Sunbeam trolleybuses continued at Moorfield Road, Wolverhampton. These were later made by Guy at Fallings Park until the end of the trolleybus era.

It was not all closures, for after the AJS liquidation the Stevens brothers moved back to their original Retreat Street works and brought out a light three-wheel delivery van. This was designed by Harry Stevens and some five hundred were sold. There was also a range of Stevens motorcycles of which about two hundred a year were produced until 1938. At this time all vehicle production ceased, because of large general engineering orders received from the re-armament programme.

The Clarke business ceased production of Wolf motorcycles in around 1925; the Waine family took over the company and moved to Colliery Road, Wolverhampton, manufacturing the Wolf motorcycle from 1930 to 1939, and continuing production of Wearwell cycles until the 1950s.

By 1939 most of the vehicle industry had left the Black Country though Guy Motors, acquired by the British Motor Corporation, continued until 1978. After the war there was something of a small scale resurgence with several scooters and sports cars being made in Wolverhampton. Jensen at West Bromwich continued to make specialist, luxury cars with fluctuating success, into the 1990s.

The last Norton Commando motorcycles were made at Villiers' Wolverhampton works. Over two million engines for motorcycles and industrial purposes had been produced there, the last Commando in 1978.

The only vehicle production in the Black Country in 1995 is in the shape of kit cars, with the excellent Kingswinford-based Westfield the best known. At Cradley Heath the popular three-wheel Lomax is built along with the Rickman Ranger. Finding many adherents is the Quantum from Stourbridge.

The Black Country is still very important for the manufacture of motor vehicle components. John Thompson Motor Pressings at Bilston makes large numbers of chassis for a range of customers. The gigantic Goodyear Tyre and Rubber Company came to Wolverhampton in 1927 and is still a major employer and leader in its field. Perhaps not now known for its motor industry connections, IMI Marston can trace its origins directly back to John Marston. They maintain a fine Heritage Centre at their Wolverhampton works.

There should soon be further opportunities for Black Country skills to be employed again in motor vehicle component manufacture in the vast automotive parts park that is being developed by the Black Country Development Corporation on the site of the former Patent Shaft Works at Wednesbury.

In a book about Black Country road vehicles it is appropriate to mention Tarmac, one of the great public works contractors and builders of roads, which has its headquarters in this area.

Another local road-related innovation was the installation in November 1927 of the country's first automatic traffic signals in Prince's Square, Wolverhampton. These came about after a visit by the Borough's Chief Constable, David Webster, to Germany where some were already operating. His successor, Edwin Tilley, also keen to solve increasing traffic problems, introduced tubular barriers on pavements at busy crossings. These became know as 'Tilley's Tubes' or 'pens for pedestrians'.

Although what is left of the British Motor Industry is located elsewhere, there remains in the Black Country great pride in the achievements of the superb engineering craftsmen of the first half of the twentieth century. Tribute should be paid to those who have preserved examples of those engineers' works, which continue to interest people who attend in their thousands rallies of vintage and veteran vehicles.

Jim Boulton, 1995.

Wolf motorcycles were offered with Villiers' engines from 1930 to 1939, and were priced from £15 5s to £34.

BICYCLES & HORSE-DRAWN VEHICLES

A velocipede made by Forder of Wolverhampton. Here

Alfred Forder, of the well-known coachbuilders, is seen

on a machine on which he achieved some success in

cycle races at Molyneux Grounds in 1869.

A Cogent tricycle, *c*. 1870. Bessie Clarke is on a machine manufactured by Henry Clarke, who built up a substantial business from 1869.

A specially built Cogent tricycle for a Mr Panter who had lost a leg in the Crimean War (1853–6). He is seen here with Jack Clarke of Cogent Works, Darlington Street, Wolverhampton.

Baruch Beckley on a Sunbeam bicycle. He already had a cycle repair shop at 31 Dudley Road, Brierley Hill, established in 1888. On 30 September 1898 he was awarded the first Sunbeam Cycle Agency. When aged forty-three he won for the fourth time Wolverhampton Wheelers Twelve Hour Road Race. For twenty-three years he held the record for the Stourbridge to Manchester race. His business became Beckley's Garage; Mr Beckley was joined by sons Fred in 1916 and Ebenezer in 1922. The family sold the business in 1965.

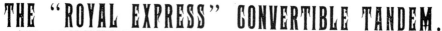

THE "ROYAL EXPRESS" CONVERTIBLE TANDEM.

EASILY CONVERTED INTO A SINGLE MACHINE.

PRICE £22.

Fitted with patent front wheel brake, ball bearings to all wheels and cranks, Harrington's double-action cradle springs, bright parts nickel-plated, remainder enamelled. Complete with lamp, saddles, valise, spanner, oilcan and bell.

MAKER: JOSEPH DEVEY, THE ASHES, WOLVERHAMPTON.
London Agents: HUTCHINS, HAMILTON & CO, 115, Queen Victoria Street, E.C.

This Joseph Devey advertisement of 1886 is from his second period as a cycle-maker. He first commenced manufacture in 1870, later sold out to Humber, and then started up again.

A two-wheel baker's van outside Pettit's store, Stafford Street, Wolverhampton, *c.* 1900. Mr Pettit is on the right behind the delivery man and behind his dog.

A two-wheel laundry van made by Edward Evans, Motor Body and Coach Builder, Steppingstone Street, Dudley, for the Belgrave Steam Laundry, Dudley, *c.* 1904.

Part of Smethwick Laundry's fleet of vans, *c.* 1904.

HORACE NICHOLLS,

High-class Wheelwright and Coachbuilder,

MANUFACTURER OF

BUILDERS' and other IRONWORK.

REPAIRS

Neatly executed in all Branches.

ESTIMATES AND DESIGNS FREE.

H. N. begs to call attention to these Up-to-date Carriage Works, where every description of Two and Four-wheel Business and Pleasure Vehicles are built to order and kept in stock; and also wishes to draw special attention to the fact that he is the only Carriage Builder in the Town that fixes Rubber Tyres on the premises, and by sending your Vehicles to the undermentioned address you SAVE MIDDLEMEN'S PROFITS.

Agent for Dunlop and North British Motor Tyres.

Note Address—POTTERS LANE CARRIAGE WORKS, WEDNESBURY.

An advertisement for Wednesbury coachbuilder, Horace Nicholls, 1909. Note the reference to motor tyres.

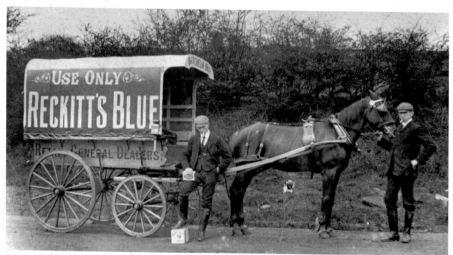

A four-wheel cart made by Edward Evans for general dealers Batchelor Brothers of Dudley, seen here *c.* 1906. Reckitt's Blue was used to whiten the wash and also as a wasp sting antidote.

A two-wheel van for Poole's Bakery, High Street, Dudley, made by Edward Evans in 1907.

A brewer's dray for Banks & Co., Park Brewery, Wolverhampton, in Edward Evans' Pitfield Street, Dudley, paint shop, 1907.

An early *Express & Star* newspaper delivery van. The photograph was taken when the van was exhibited in the 1949 local Cavalcade of Transport.

Wolverhampton horse-drawn bus 'Wulfruna'.

MOTOR CARS

A 1921 16 h.p. four-cylinder Sunbeam tourer, price £1,125. The driver is thought to be Charles Marston.

An Electric Construction Company battery-powered vehicle. This Wolverhampton company's brilliant electrical engineer, Thomas Parker, seated centre, designed several such vehicles, and commuted to business in the one illustrated.

An 1897 petrol car being tested on a 1 in 6 gradient at the ECC's Bushbury works.

Star Motor Car

Price from 160 Guineas

WITH

Clipper Tyres.

$3\frac{1}{2}$ h.p.

— ·

WRITE FOR OUR ILLUSTRATED
LIST AND TESTIMONIALS.

Design A.

Why is the Star Motor the best of its class ?

BECAUSE—You have not to push up hills. *See report on Hill-climbing Contest—* Taddington Hill at the rate of nine miles per hour, Birkhill eight miles per hour.

BECAUSE—It is a Gentleman's Carriage, *not a seat on four wheels.*

BECAUSE—Intending purchasers can always test a car on country roads and up hills of one in ten gradient—*not on London asphalt.*

BECAUSE—It is exceptionally silent when travelling—*not like a reaping machine at work.*

BECAUSE—It is all made at our Works, Wolverhampton. *The longer it is used the better it becomes.*

BECAUSE—It is simplicity itself and can be manipulated by anyone.

BECAUSE—*it is free from complicated machinery.*

BECAUSE—The speed of Motor is 700 revolutions per minute—*not 2,000, tearing itself to bits.*

BECAUSE—It is kept cool by water, *not air*, this is the most effectual and reliable method.

BECAUSE—All competitors have to acknowledge its superiority as a hill-climber, and *it is only $3\frac{1}{4}$ h.p.*

BECAUSE—It is the most economical Car yet produced.

BECAUSE—F. S. Edge, one of our greatest authorities on Motoring, states the Star to be *the best Car of its class yet produced.* See "Wheeling," March 28th 1900.

STAR MOTOR CO., Stewart St., Wolverhampton

An advertisement for the Star Motor Company, 1900. The twelve reasons given why it is the best in its class make entertaining reading.

The second Sunbeam car, 1900. It had a 4 h.p. single-cylinder engine, and belt and spur gear transmission with two speeds and reverse Crypto gear. It did not go into production.

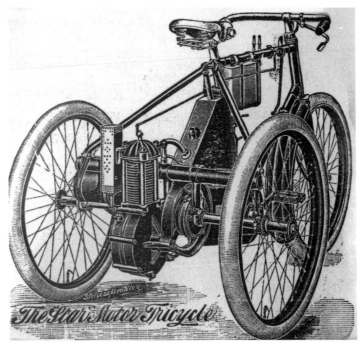

An 1899 Star motor tricycle based on the popular De Dion model. Motor tricycles sold well in the early days of motoring.

This 1900 Star car is said to have been the first automobile in West Bromwich. The photograph was taken at the owner Mr Thomas Gibbons' Hill Top home.

Star voiturette, February 1902. At the wheel sits Arthur Roberts, popular music hall figure of the day. The location, Wolverhampton's West Park, was very popular with photographers.

A 1901 Quad Sociable made by F.W. Trusselle, Byrne Road, Wolverhampton. It had a 2¾ h.p. De Dion engine and covered 1,000 miles in its first year. The Trusselle family was well known in the local motor trade, with a garage on the Newhampton Road until the 1950s.

Sunbeam Mabley. This strange vehicle, introduced in 1901, had a 2¾ h.p. front-mounted De Dion engine, two speeds, belt drive, and four wheels arranged in diamond formation. About 150 were sold at £140 each.

THE SENSATION OF THE NATIONAL SHOW.

THE 1903 SUNBEAM CAR.

Four cylinders.

12 h.p.

NO NOISE.   NO VIBRATION.   500 Guineas.

Catalogue free, describing special features. . . .

JOHN MARSTON. LTD.. Moorfield Motor Works, WOLVERHAMPTON

The Sunbeam of 1903, which had a French Berliet engine. From 1904 engines and most components of Sunbeam vehicles were made by Sunbeam themselves.

The 1904 Little Star. This photograph of Samuel Johnson and family was taken in 1914. Samuel was a photographer in Victoria Passage, Stourbridge. He later built up a coach business in that town, Supreme Coaches, which operated until it was taken over by Don Everall in the 1970s.

Sunbeam 12/14. This car, driven by Fred Eastmead, took part in 1904 in a demonstration run from Land's End to John O'Groats and back without an engine stop.

Louis Coatalen's first design for Sunbeam, 1909. The brilliant French designer is at the wheel. In the back seat is Edward Genner, who later made LVL commercial vehicles in Wolverhampton.

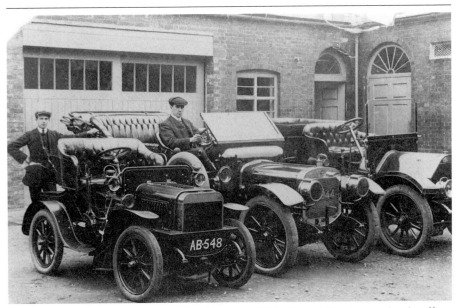

Sir Henry and Lady Grey's cars at Enville Hall, 1920. Richard Smallman, the chauffeur, is at the wheel of the Sunbeam. A Humber is on the right of the photograph, a Wolseley on the left. Richard's brother Harold, assistant chauffeur, is standing.

Star 21.1 h.p. five-seat tourer, 1914. With streamlined body, 'bull-nosed' radiator, hood, windscreen and dynamo, this car was priced at £460.

A 1911 10 h.p. Briton Doctor's Victoria. This twin-cylinder car with hood and windscreen, made by Star, sold for £215.

A Briton four-cylinder car. With hood, windscreen and torpedo bodywork it was listed at £320. West Park was the location for the photograph. Britons were made as a low priced range of cars to complement Star's other model range.

Crescent cycle-car, 1912. With V-twin JAP engine and friction drive, this model (seen here with Mrs Hartley Smith at the wheel) cost £127. The manufacturer started in Walsall in 1911 but soon moved to Smethwick.

A 1914 Universal coupé produced by Turner's Motor Manufacturing Company, Lever Street, Wolverhampton, for the Universal Motor Co., Piccadilly. It cost £250.

A 1912 Medinger cycle car. Designed by Emile Medinger, a member of Sunbeam's racing team, this machine was powered by a twin-cylinder two-stroke engine. A speed of 60 m.p.h. was claimed for this prototype, which never went into production because of the outbreak of war.

The New British Cyclecar, 1921–3. Made by Charles Willetts & Son, Cradley Heath, better known for lifting gear, this model was powered by an 8 h.p. V-twin Blackburne engine with friction transmission. About a hundred were made, costing £210 each.

A 1911 Sunbeam 25–30 double landaulette used as a taxi by H.W. Boulton, Penn Garage, Wolverhampton. When new it cost £740, but when auctioned in 1925 the car only realized £25.

Sunbeam 20 h.p. ohv six-cylinder saloon, listed at £760. This photograph was taken at the Sunbeam playing fields in 1931.

A 1934 25 h.p. Sunbeam seven-seater limousine. Listed at £1,045, the road tax, then determined by horsepower, would have been £24.

Sunbeam 'Dawn' 12.8 h.p. saloon, 1934. With four-cylinder ohv engine, independent front suspension and a four-speed pre-selector gear box this model was priced at £480. Annual road tax would have cost £13.

Sunbeam limousine. This vehicle, with special coachwork, was designed and built in the Sunbeam factory for the Duke of Gloucester in about 1932.

A Ford saloon fitted with the first set of Goodyear Airwheels (9.00–13), at the Wolverhampton factory, March 1932. The tyres were fitted directly on to special hubs.

Three Ford cars and a Jensen (last in the queue). These cars were supplied by Billingham's, Wolverhampton main Ford dealer, and they are seen here turning into Waterloo Road en route for the 1935 Silver Jubilee celebrations. The Jensen was West Bromwich-made and had a Ford V8 engine.

A 1936 Vauxhall saloon with David Turpin, who had a considerable haulage business at Charles Street, Willenhall, and was also a racehorse owner.

An early ABC tricar. These were made in small numbers by Ken Heather and Bill Powell of Auto Bodycraft at Pensnett in the early 1970s. Based on reconditioned Mini mechanicals the cost was £400. The road tax was only £10, as the car was a three-wheeler.

Jensen Interceptor, 1973. This West Bromwich-made luxury car had a 7.2-litre Chrysler V8 engine and cost some £7,000. Production at this time was eighteen a week; in a production life of seventeen years almost 4,500 were sold.

A 3½ h.p. Star, 1900. Owner Mr S.R. Rhodes, seen here with his wife, was a prominent Wolverhampton solicitor and a pioneer motorist. Once Secretary of Wolverhampton Tricycling Club, he was also first secretary of Wolverhampton & District Automobile Club in 1901.

A 1903 16 h.p. Ariel tonneau. DA 1, Wolverhampton's first motor vehicle registration – introduced on 1 January 1904 – was allocated to this car. It belonged to Mr S.R. Rhodes.

Mr S.R. Rhodes' Ariel, thought to be at The Hermitage, Bridgnorth, at the Wolverhampton Club's Hill Climb, *c.* 1904.

A 1921 15.9 h.p. Humber saloon, also carrying the DA 1 registration.

In 1924 Mr Rhodes still had the same registration on his Rolls-Royce 20. Mr and Mrs Rhodes are accompanied by their daughter and a Mr J.P. Wood.

DA 1 on a 1949 Mark 1 Sunbeam Talbot. The registration is still with the Rhodes family, one of only six families in the country to retain their original number.

Section Three

MOTORCYCLES

*Baruch Beckley on a Sunbeam motorcycle. Beckley's Garage, Dudley Road, Brierley Hill,
developed from Baruch's original cycle repair shop at no. 31, with large premises also on
the opposite side of the road. Here for some years the Urban District fire engines and
ambulance were kept and maintained.*

Omega powered bicycle, 1909. Of ingenious design and with a 1½ h.p. motor, this was an attempt to popularize the powered bicycle. At £26 for a lady's or gent's model, few were sold. The gentlemen are thought to be R.S. Roberts and S. Dorsett, who later made the successful Diamond motorcycles.

An AJS Sociable motorcycle combination and Mr and Mrs Jack Clarke of the Wearwell Cycle Company, *c.* 1914. This machine was driven from the sidecar.

Clyno staff outing to Stourport, 1915. They were photographed near the Pelham Street works; Brickkiln Street School is in the background. The Clyno Company's founding cousins were present, Frank in a Peugeot (extreme left), Alwyn in a Panhard (extreme right).

A 1920 De Luxe motorcycle assembled by A.E. Bradford, who later became well known as owner of Motorities, Wolverhampton. This model had a James V-twin engine.

Ariel motorcycle, 1920s. The disc wheels were something of a fad at this time, but affected steering in crosswinds. The rider here, Billy Walters, came from Brierley Hill.

The Pen Nib. This machine was built in around 1922 with a Royal Ruby engine by H.W. (Bill) Boulton, seen here, who owned Penn Garage, Lloyd Hill, Wolverhampton.

A two-stroke Pen Nib model, *c.* 1920. It was photographed at Bill Boulton's original garage on the corner of Church Hill and Penn Road. Pen Nibs had tanks shaped to resemble a J nib.

Arthur Rock of Rock & Son on a 1921 Rockson motorcycle. The company was a Cradley Heath iron and steel firm which made some 400 machines between 1920 and 1923, half of which went to India.

A Sharratt combination made at Carter's Green, West Bromwich. Gordon and Gilbert Sharratt are on this JAP V-twin powered outfit.

Hybrid Sunbeam, based on a Model 90 racer. This photograph shows 'Bunny' Jeavons at Trescott Grange. Note the plus-fours, popular men's wear at the time.

AJS machines out on test at Enville, c. 1925. Clarrie Wise is on the combination and George Stevens' daughter Millie rides the solo.

DMW 'Bambi' scooters, with a 98 cc Villiers engine and two-speed gear, at High Green, Tettenhall, 1958. About five hundred machines were made at Sedgley and sold for £110.

A 1957 Hermes scooter made by Mercury Industries (Birmingham) at Dock Lane, Dudley and Pool Street, Wolverhampton. Priced at £85 5s, few were sold.

A Villiers-powered sidecar outfit driven by Bert Kershaw, 'Mr Villiers' to the industry, leaving the Marston Road works watched by Jim Finlan, Security Officer, in 1957.

The two millionth Villiers engine was handed over by Geoffrey Jones, Joint Managing Director, to C.F. Caunter of the South Kensington Science Museum in 1956.

VILLIERS

TWO-STROKE ENGINES KNOCK OUT COMPLICATIONS.

PREVENTION

is better than cure—elimination is better than adjustment. That is why the VILLIERS TWO-STROKE Engine scores heavily.

It is not handicapped with a multiplicity of components, but has only 3 moving parts, rendering it supremely efficient, simple, easy to start, and cheap in upkeep. It is built to last and is a complete unit for POWER and LIGHT which for economy has no equal.

Write for Illustrated Booklet.

VILLIERS ENGINEERING CO., LTD.,
MARSTON ROAD - - WOLVERHAMPTON.

This advertisement of 1924 extols the virtues of the two-stroke Villiers engine.

Section Four

AMBULANCES, FIRE ENGINES & VOLUNTEERS

A 1914 Star ambulance at the Royal Hospital, Wolverhampton, c. 1930. In the picture, uniformed, are, left to right: Inspector William Edwards, Third Officer William Penn (both of the Police Force Fire Brigade), Inspector Albert Jones, PC W77 Jim Jones (said to be Wolverhampton's tallest policeman).

The Sunbeam ambulance presented to the Red Cross by The Reform Club in 1915.

Two 1914 Dennis fire appliances and a 1914 Star ambulance at Red Lion Street, Wolverhampton, mid-1920s. Chief Fire Officer Sam Penn is in the middle vehicle with William Edwards, later Chief Fire Officer, standing. The wheeled escape was added in 1921.

Wolverhampton's Dennis fire appliance of 1914, to which the wheeled escape was added in 1921. The helmeted passenger is Chief Fire Officer Sam Penn.

Dudley's 1926 60 h.p. Leyland fire appliance.

A Leyland fire appliance dating from the mid-1930s in its later life, as part of F.H. Lloyd's Works Fire Brigade.

Seen here on its return from one of Wolverhampton's biggest fires, at Hickman's Monmore Green timber yard, August 1949, is a Ford fire appliance of the Goodyear Works Fire Brigade.

Left to right: Commer, Austin, Ford and Bedford fire appliances at Tettenhall fire station, early 1950s.

Morris Commercial, Austin and Ford ambulances at Penn Road Station, 1949. The site is now occupied by a temple. Left to right: Fireman Sam Silcock, Station Officer Alan Smith, Chief Fire and Ambulance Officer J.G. Jessop, R.G. Keeley, his Deputy.

This is a rare photograph of an LVL (Light Vehicles Limited) product, which was given its hearse bodywork by L. & L.T. Taylor for the Wolverhampton Board of Guardians.

The 1925 20 h.p. Austin ambulance supplied to Dudley Borough. It was fitted with two stretchers, internal heating and first aid equipment.

A 1927 Star 20/60 ambulance which was supplied to Hallam Hospital, Sheffield. It was paid for by a local 'Penny in the Pound Fund'. This was a scheme which deducted money from workers' wages to raise funds for local hospitals. The photograph was taken behind the Star coachbuilding department at Bushbury.

A 1949 Wolseley police car, belonging to Wolverhampton Borough Force.

Astride this 1953 BSA A7 is Wolverhampton PC Joe Davies, wearing a 'Corker' helmet. The machine has a Phoenix screen. Joe served for twenty-two years and retired as a Superintendent. He is well known locally as he travels with his Lady Wulfruna mechanical organ in aid of charities.

1959 DKR Pegasus scooters being evaluated for police duties. Left to right: WPC Blossom Timmins, Inspector P.D. Peterson, Jimmy Goodall (DKR Sales Manager), WPS Monica Taylor, Chief Constable Norman Goodchild OBE.

"STAR" WAR LORRY AS SUPPLIED
TO THE BRITISH & RUSSIAN GOVERNMEN

A 50 cwt Star lorry as supplied to various Allied Governments in the First World War.
Note the large spotlight and fire extinguisher.

The departure of Wolverhampton Volunteer Rifle Corps to camp at Burwarton from Chapel Ash, August 1915, with two Sunbeams and a Rolls-Royce.

Two early Guys, the baggage wagons for the Burwarton camp. This marque was established in 1914.

A Sunbeam tourer with Transport Officer F.F. Sharpe.

The motorcycle section at Burwarton. Nearest to the camera is a Wolverhampton-registered Indian twin.

Six-wheeled Vickers Guy armoured cars for the Indian Army, at the Fallings Park works.

Front view of a Vickers Guy armoured car. These vehicles were later converted to artillery tractors.

Section Five

COMMERCIAL
VEHICLES

A 1917 Austin lorry. This vehicle had one propshaft to each rear wheel. It is shown out-
side the premises of W.J. Smith, coachbuilders. Note the poster advertising the appearance
of a Chinese (actually American) conjuror, whose illusion included catching a fired bullet
on a plate. During a London show it all went wrong and Ching died in hospital.

Star 15/20 h.p. 30/40 cwt lorry, 1914. The company built many commercial vehicles. This example also has a Star body made for W. Butler & Co., Brewers. The chassis price was £445.

Star 2-ton van with Star body, 1914. This one belonged to W.H. Weaver, well-known and old established Wolverhampton provision merchants.

A 1914 Star 10 cwt light delivery van outside Craddocks, a large Wolverhampton footwear business.

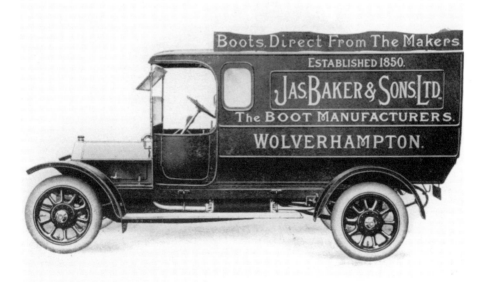

Used by another Wolverhampton footwear manufacturer and merchant, this is a 1914 Star 1-ton van with Star bodywork.

1914 Star 50 cwt lorries. These are seen setting off from the Frederick Street works to a Pratt's depot.

Near the works, this 1917 Star lorry awaits delivery to a well-known brewer – Ind Coope.

A 1914 Hallford lorry, with Edward Evans bodywork, built for J.V. Wood of Grange Road Mill.

A 1914 Daimler van bodied by Edward Evans for Vono of Dudley Port. Note the spare wheel bolted to the rear wheel.

A 1920 Daimler van bodied by Smith of West Bromwich for Goodwin, Foster, Brown of Dudley, provision merchants noted for their self-raising flour.

Owned by Wolverhampton's leading furniture remover, Ernest Hodgetts Ltd, this is a mid-1920s AEC vehicle.

A 1947 Guy Vixen 4-ton pantechnicon, which did sterling work for Ernest Hodgetts Ltd.

J.N. Miller operated this mid-1930s Beardmore Multi-wheeler. Miller's, of Corn Hill, Wolverhampton, had a 300-year history.

An Albion tipper truck operated by J.N. Miller in the 1960s.

Harry Farmer, Thomas Street, Wolverhampton, used Model T Ford lorries to collect milk in churns. Here are George and Ambrose Farmer with a 1924 Model T.

Three Bedford lorries owned by David Turpin of Charles Street, Willenhall. Note the L plate: these were introduced in 1935.

A 1925 Star 25 cwt van with Star bodywork. This was used for the delivery of W.D. & H.O. Wills' publicity material.

This finely sign-written Guy six-wheel van, *c.* 1935, was owned by Chivers, a famous Histon, Cambridgeshire, company.

A 1935 Morris Commercial van. Wolverhampton Steam Laundry, established 1890, ran large fleets of these vans in red and white livery. This example was bodied by Smith of West Bromwich.

Bodied by Smith of West Bromwich, this 1935 Commer van was for Supreme Laundries of Smethwick. Note the price charged for laundry work.

A 1935 forward control Ford V8 van bodied by Comer of Bilston. H. Beach and Son, an old-established firm, is still in business.

Morris Commercial forward control van, bodied by Smith of West Bromwich for James Beattie Ltd, Wolverhampton's leading department store, established in 1867 and still going strong.

Wolverhampton Box Company, est. 1922, operated this well sign-written 1937 Morris Commercial pantechnicon. The firm was later part of Bryant & May.

An early 1930s 3–4 ton Karrier. This was used by H.P. Miers, est. 1925, whose main business, before the use of tankers, was the collection of milk in churns.

A 1935 Armstrong Saurer van. Of Swiss origin, these vehicles were built in Newcastle on Tyne, under licence.

Operated by a Birmingham contractor for Goodyear, as was the van above, this is a 1934 forward control Commer.

A 1933 Jowett. This twin-cylinder van, noted for its reliability and economy and made at Idle, Bradford, was used by Goodyear for local light deliveries.

Goodyear ran a fleet of these Bedford CA vans. This example dates from 1953.

A mid-1930s forward control Guy pantechnicon.

This 1938 Guy 'Wolf' belonged to Aymer Barrow of Lower Horseley Field and Railway Drive, Wolverhampton, scrap and coal merchants.

A 1934 forward control Commer van, bodied by Smith of West Bromwich, and used by Martin Dunn Ltd, High Street, West Bromwich.

This 1934 Bedford lorry with Smith body was used by Birmid of Smethwick, large-scale suppliers of castings to the motor industry.

A 1933 Fordson 2-ton lorry. Himley Bricks used some local haulage contractors; Alec Finlow of High Street, Pensnett, was one of them.

Also operated for Himley Bricks, but by Hughes Brothers of Lower Gornal, was this 1935 Thornycroft lorry.

Costing approximately £200, this 1933 Bedford 2–3 ton lorry was used by leading Wolverhampton fruit and potato merchant R.A. Walley.

A Thornycroft brewer's dray used by Butler's Brewery, Wolverhampton, *c.* 1935.

An American Reo Speedwagon, *c.* 1933. Few foreign lorries were seen pre-war but some American vehicles, such as this, gained favour. The operator was Smith & Griffiths, Halesowen Road, Old Hill.

Dating from the same period, a forward control Reo Speedwagon, operated by Smith & Griffiths. Note the Stafford Knott emblem on their vehicles.

Seen with its owner, J. Collins of Stourbridge, this 1936 American Diamond T4.5 would have cost about £430.

A 1936 Fordson V8 lorry, British-built, and Dudley-registered with Horace Orford of Tansey Green, Pensnett.

A First World War Maudsley. This vehicle was operated by Joseph Male of Pensnett. Founded in 1919 by Joseph Male, this large firm is still in business. Here, driver B. Malpass is seen road-making on the Hawbush Estate, Brierley Hill, in the late 1920s.

This Leyland 'Beaver' tractor unit with ergomatic cab was introduced in 1964. It is seen here with an industrial locomotive load in Dreadnought Road, Pensnett.

Late 1950s ERF lorry. This wide load is a pit cage, one of many made by Allens of Tipton. Joseph Male, the haulier, was a very influential and respected figure in the road haulage business, as was his son Jack, who held high office in the Road Haulage Association.

Bunkers Hill Bakery of Bilston owned the horse-drawn van, built by Comer of Bilston, and the Ford Y van belonged to Fosters of Cannock, World Champion Bakers, 1919–23. The photograph dates from the mid-1930s.

Hickmans & Mould were a large dairy business with premises in Westbury Street, Wolverhampton. This electric milk float dates from *c.* 1937.

The 1914 AJS sidecar outfit was seen as an economical delivery vehicle, and this example cost £88 10s. It was made at the Retreat Street AJS factory.

Turner two-stroke 148 cc Byvan, *c.* 1949. This was another motorcycle-based commercial, costing £120. Stan Simmons is putting tools into a capacious goods space while his boss Richard Lee looks on.

These lorries, mostly Leylands, belonged to J. Cross & Sons, Willenhall Road, Wolverhampton, quarry owners and transport contractors. The photograph was taken in 1932.

The fleet of J. Cross & Sons was mostly Bedfords by 1937. The third and fourth from the left in the front row are Commers.

Sentinel DG 6 wagons (double-geared, six-wheeled), assembled at the Shrewsbury Works in 1928 before delivery to Tarmac, Wolverhampton's great public works company.

A Ford 'D' lorry with special telescopic body services a Barber Green finisher on a Tarmac contract, *c.* 1952.

Renault, Standard, Clyno and Morris cars, with Guy and Morris lorries, 1933. This is the fleet of Wolverhampton manufacturing chemists, Reade Brothers, Cleveland Road.

This was Wolverhampton Steam Laundry's fleet of Morris Commercial vans at their Sweetman Street Laundry, 1928. The vans were immaculate in their red and white livery. Note the 'Economy Wash' sign on the first van.

Commer vans used for the delivery of the *Express & Star*, mid-1930s.

The fleet of W.B. Tatlow and Son, Plumbers, Cleveland Road, Wolverhampton, 1959.
There is one BMC vehicle; all the rest are Fords.

A Foden eight-wheeler, 1956. This was one of a considerable fleet operated by Horace Kendrick, Mary Street, Walsall, and used on bulk coal transport.

This NCB coal tanker is on a Ford Trader chassis. These were introduced to allow coal to be delivered as easily as oil, via pipes.

Section Six

PUBLIC PASSENGER

VEHICLES

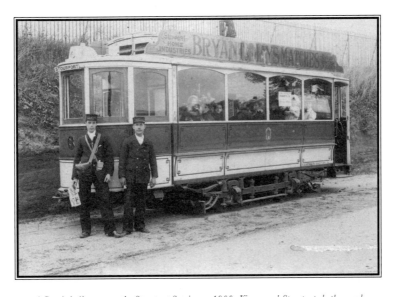

A Brush-built tram on the Stourport Service, c. 1900. Kinver and Stourport, both served

by trams, were popular destinations for Black Country folk. The conductor's paper is the

once-popular 'Chips' comic.

A tramcar of the South Staffs Tramcar Company passing Darlaston generating station, 1894. All of the electrical equipment was made by the Electric Construction Corporation under the supervision of Thomas Parker.

This battery-powered fourteen-seat bus with four-wheel steering, four-wheel brakes and four-wheel drive was made by the Electric Construction Company in around 1897 at Bushbury works. (The company name changed in 1896.)

Wolseley motor bus, Wolverhampton Corporation Transport. Three were operated from October 1905, until replaced by trams in 1909.

Single-decker bus of the Birmingham & Midland Motor Omnibus Company at Kingswinford Cross, 1926. The conductor, Jim Tyler, was Midland Welterweight Boxing Champion, and there were no fare dodgers on his bus. He later became an Inspector.

Sunbeam single-decker 'Pathan' motor bus. Few of this model were produced. Wolverhampton Corporation Transport operated two for the Bridgnorth route in around 1931. Note the ladder and the luggage rack on the roof.

A 1937 Guy double-decker takes up passengers at Wombourne Church during the last war. The fine manor house and the wall surrounding it have long since gone.

Brand new from coachbuilders W. David Smith, West Bromwich, this is the Corporation Transport 1934 28-seater Dennis, no. 34.

Sunbeam MS2 trolleybus with Weymann body. This vehicle entered service at Walsall in October 1933 and was withdrawn in 1956.

Star charabanc, 1914. With a torpedo body this 25-seater cost £710 new. It was photographed on the A449 at Ashwood. Note the gipsy caravan in the background.

Daimler charabanc. This 1920 model was one of the first for Samuel Johnson with a W.J. Smith body.

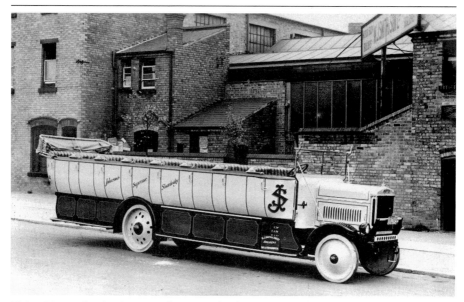

This 1925 Leyland RAF GH6 for Samuel Johnson, Supreme Coaches, Victoria Passage, Stourbridge, was bodied by W.J. Smith.

Another Samuel Johnson vehicle: A 1927 ADC 32-seater charabanc. For a short time there was an association between Daimler and the Associated Equipment Company, hence the name ADC (Associated Daimler Company).

Wolverhampton Market, 1920s; St Peter's Church is in the background. The front row shows Guys belonging to Tours & Transport of King Street. The wholesale (left) and retail (right) markets have long since gone.

This 1925 Hallford charabanc belonged to Tours & Transport, and the photograph was by Bennett Clarke.

AEC charabanc, *c*. 1922. This was the start of an outing from the Beehive Inn, Great Bridge, to Evesham.

Talbot with 14-seat body by W.J. Smith, West Bromwich. This was operated by Invincible Coaches, Birmingham.

AJS Commodore 30-seat coach, with Buckingham body, registered in April 1930 and operated by Hill's Tours, West Bromwich.

A 1931 AJS Pilot 25 h.p. coach. This vehicle had a six-cylinder Meadows engine and a Birlington body. It was made for Leamington Touring Services, which was based at Blackpool.

This 1927 Star Flyer was operated by Holden's of Griffin Street, Netherton, and William Holden is at the wheel. So good did this vehicle prove to be that other local firms bought the model.

An early 1930s Guy coach, operated by Tours & Transport of King Street, Wolverhampton. It is seen here on a country excursion.

David Turpin of Willenhall operated his early 1920s Chevrolet as a lorry during the week, and with a change of body (shown) as a coach at the weekend.

A small Bean bus, *c.* 1930. J.T. Field & Son of Dudley operated this vehicle, one of Bean's considerable number of commercial vehicles.

This 1925 Leyland coach belonged to A. Walsgrove's Throstle Luxury Tours, Loake Road, West Bromwich, and was bodied by W. David Smith of the same town.

These two coaches – a Daimler with Birlington Seagull body and a Maudsley – belonged to Harman's Motor Services, Compton Road, Wolverhampton.

Many motor coaches ended up as works transport. This Leyland bus was used for that purpose by M.A. Boswell, Wolverhampton public works contractor.

The Turner LDV Rixi of *c.* 1950 was conceived as a motorized rickshaw for the Far East. This example was operated by Bob's Taxis, North Street, Wolverhampton.

COMPETITION VEHICLES

Sunbeam ohv sprint machine (just post-First World War) ridden by the legendary George Dance, a superb sprinter and tuner. Note the lack of protective gear. George is seen changing gear and would have reached 80 m.p.h.

A 1912 Star 'Comet' single-seater racing car. This was raced at Brooklands with some success. It is seen here outside the Frederick Street works with Dick Lisle at the wheel.

A 1919 Sunbeam 4.9 litre Indianapolis car, fitted with single-seater body, and seen here at Brooklands on 24 May 1920. Two handicap races were won at 98.15 m.p.h. and 101.25 m.p.h.

The first British supercharged racing cars in Sunbeam's experimental shop. DA 8420, driven by Henry Segrave, won the 1924 Spanish Grand Prix. DA 8666 was still winning at Brooklands in 1929 when driven by local driver E.L. Bouts.

Sunbeam 'Tigress', Brooklands, 1929. Alec Broome, later well known as the owner of Conway Service Station, Fighting Cocks, Wolverhampton, is painting the numbers. Frank Bill is in the white overalls.

The SUPREME SUNBEAM

1,000 H.P. CAR.
BUILT BY
THE SUNBEAM MOTOR CAR C? LT?
WOLVERHAMPTON
ENGLAND

207 *M.P.H.*
Timed over a 5 Kilometre course
March 29th 1927

The 1,000 h.p. Sunbeam that was driven by Henry Segrave in a successful World Land Speed Record Attempt on 29 March 1927, for which he was knighted.

The 1,000 h.p. Sunbeam on the Wolverhampton Cavalcade of Transport, 2 April 1949. Owned by Humber of Coventry, it is seen on a low loader belonging to Wright Brothers of Crown Street. The car is now at the National Motor Museum, Beaulieu.

Sunbeam Cub racer. At the 1958 Sunbeam Register Rally, this car was driven by the PRO of the Rootes Group (its owners), with famous *Motor Sport* editor Bill Boddy as passenger.

Turner 2 litre Formula 2 sports car, driven by John Webb at the Prescott Hill Climb, 1955.

Kieft Formula 3 (500 cc). One of the few racing cars built by Cyril Kieft, South Wales steel magnate, this Norton-powered car is being driven by Ken Wharton, Smethwick garage owner.

A 1914 Isle of Man Junior TT winner Eric Williams (no. 27); AJS team mate Cyril Williams (no. 20) was second. This was the first big racing success for AJS.

The 1922 AJS TT Races team. On the left is George Rowley, a great all-rounder who spent all his working life with AJS, and second from right is Clarrie Wise. No luxury mobile homes were available then for the competitors.

Two Sharratt riders setting off for a reliability trial from Carter's Green, *c*. 1925.

Kaye Don with his 1921 Diamond at Brooklands in 1921.

Vivian Prestwich on the machine on which he set a new Flying Kilo record of 69.23 m.p.h. at Brooklands on 16 April 1921.

Howard R. Davies made some eight hundred HRD machines at Fryer Street, Wolverhampton, until 1927 after achieving successes with Sunbeam and AJS. He won the 1925 Senior TT and here is shown arriving at Douglas on a 1925 HRD for the 1926 races in which he retired, the best HRD finishing fifth.

The AJS 350 cc trials team, 1926. Left to right: Clarrie Wise, L.R. Coen, Leo Davenport. They won the 1926 Manufacturers 350 cc Team Prize and the Scottish Six Days event.

Sunbeam Special. This was built from 1926 works TT machine parts, and its rider is Tommy Deadman, Sunbeam tester, pioneer dirt track rider and motorcycle football star.

A 1935 Stevens motorcycle. Tommy Deadman, Stevens Brothers' ace rider, displays a trophy at the end of the successful 1935 season.

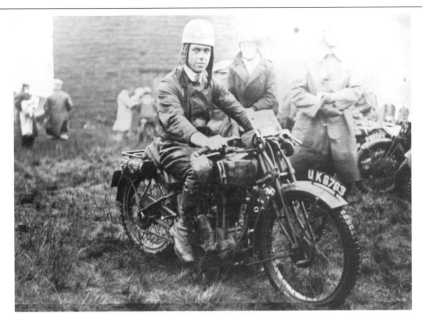

Sunbeam works rider Vic Brittain of Walsall. He was a great all-rounder and is shown here after winning the Lancashire Grand National. Later he became a Bloxwich motorcycle agent, and his sons world-class trials riders.

Sunbeam's star sidecar trials rider, N.P.O. Bradley, who won five major trials in 1929. He was owner of old established Kidderminster engineers, Bradley and Turton.

Frank Williams, Sunbeam trials team member. While Sunbeam scaled down road racing a trials team was maintained and achieved considerable success.

Sunbeam works rider Australian Arthur (Digger) Simcock after winning the 1929 Austrian Six Hours Grand Prix. He became Manager of Wolverhampton Speedway in 1950.

Section Eight

GARAGES & WORKS

The North Worcestershire Garage, Oldswinford, Stourbridge, c. 1911. The Barnes family
were the owners and successful drivers of Singer sports cars in international competitions.

Bradburn & Wedge, one of Wolverhampton's leading motor agents, 1916. The company was established in 1915 in Darlington Street. Note the white painted lamp post and masked headlights on the Sunbeam car.

Three Sunbeam cars outside Bradburn & Wedge, mid-1920s.

Barton's Coachworks, Hollyhedge Lane, Walsall, *c.* 1916.

Staffordshire Motor Tyre Company, Chapel Ash, *c.* 1925. Founded by the Fullwood family in 1908, the company became one of the largest tyre distributors in the British Isles.

Billingham's, Wolverhampton's main Ford dealer, Snow Hill showroom. Outside the showroom is the 250,000th British-made Ford. This car toured the country in 1925.

Reginald Tildesley, Willenhall's main Ford dealer, c. 1927. The Ford shown had run 1,800 miles without engine stops, and had achieved 30.5 m.p.g. Sales Manager Mr Pyatt is on the left, and Harry Bond, foreman, behind the board. The car was in use until 1943.

Penn Garage, Lloyd Hill, 1923. The sign ('Boulton's Garage') at the roadside filling station was made from the tail of a First World War fighter aircraft.

Pearshouse's Garage, South Street (later Road), Stourbridge, c. 1932. Mr N.L. Pearshouse is in the doorway. Petrol was dispensed by the swing arm over the pavement. Mechanic Fred Baker is by the pumps.

Sunbeam's Moorfield works, Blakenhall, Wolverhampton, 1908. Production was about 140 cars per annum.

The Bean works, Waddam's Pool, Dudley, *c.* 1925. About a hundred cars a week were produced here.

The Kieft works, Derry Street, Wolverhampton. Cyril Kieft is seen viewing the prototype of the 1100 cc 72 b.h.p. Coventry Climax. Weighing only 10 cwt it had a lively performance, and cost £1,599 in 1954.

DKR 'Dove' scooter production at Willenhall Motor Radiator Company's Neachells Lane works, Willenhall, 1957.

Penn Garage, corner of Penn Road and Church Hill, *c.* 1923. The Model T Ford was on a delivery run from Trafford Park.

Billingham's commercial vehicle department, Bell Street, Wolverhampton, *c.* 1947. On the left is an ex-Canadian Army Ford belonging to Bilston builders Perks & Gould, and in the centre is a Ford used by Bantocks, delivery contractors to the GWR – later BR, Western Region.

W. David Smith, West Bromwich coachbuilders, 76 High Street, *c.* 1934.

A. Comer, commercial bodybuilder, Stonefield Road, Bilston, early 1930s. This is the body shop, with a truck body on trestles.

J. Cross & Sons, 55 Willenhall Street, Wolverhampton. This photograph shows, left to right, Harry, George and Arthur Cross.

Morris Commercial 'Equiload' lorry at the Stafford Street works of well-known galvanizers, B.E. Wedge.

A Simon hydraulic platform on a Morris Commercial chassis. This was built for the GPO in 1959 by Edward Evans, Coachbuilders, Steppingstone Street, Dudley (established 1880). The founder's grandson, also Edward, is on the left with his workforce. In the background is Millard's Gipsy's Tent Brewery.

A mishap in Princes' Square, Wolverhampton. A Borough Council tower wagon has come into contact with overhead trolleybus wires. This is where the first traffic lights in Britain were installed in 1927.

Acknowledgements

Special thanks to Stan Hill, David Evans and John Bone, and thanks also to the following:

Reg Alsop • Gladys Baker • Dr Joseph Bayley • Graham Beckley • T. Bond
Alec Brew • Trina Brindley • John Butcher • Francis Cartwright • Jean Caskie
John Chambers • Albert Clarke • Vic Cox • Joe Davies • Lillian Deadman
John Dolphin • Janice Endean • Jonathan Everall • Pete Farmer • Jack Gash
Paul Gibbons • Frank Gobourne • Lorraine Harper • Claire Harrington
Ray Horton • Ray Jones • Bob Kyte • Jonathan Lewis • George Llewellyn
BEM • Ron Lucas • Mary Mills • Steve Mills • Geoff Morgan • David J. Park
Keith Parker • D.J. Roberts • Dick Rhodes • John Rhodes • Stan Simmons
Jack Spittle • Diane Spooner • Geoff Stevens • Marie Tieche
Sybille Todd-Wood • D. Turpin • J. Van Leerzem • J.A. Wigg

And to:

Wolverhampton Express & Star • Goodyear Great Britain Ltd • Tarmac PLC
Male & Son (Pensnett) Ltd • Eardley & Lewis Photographic Studio
National Motor Museum • Wolverhampton Library Local Studies Dept
Sandwell Local Studies Centre.

BRITAIN IN OLD PHOTOGRAPHS

To order any of these titles please telephone Littlehampton Book Services on 01903 721596

ALDERNEY

Alderney: A Second Selection, *B Bonnard*

BEDFORDSHIRE

Bedfordshire at Work, *N Lutt*

BERKSHIRE

Maidenhead, *M Hayles & D Hedges*
Around Maidenhead, *M Hayles & B Hedges*
Reading, *P Southerton*
Reading: A Second Selection, *P Southerton*
Sandhurst and Crowthorne, *K Dancy*
Around Slough, *J Hunter & K Hunter*
Around Thatcham, *P Allen*
Around Windsor, *B Hedges*

BUCKINGHAMSHIRE

Buckingham and District, *R Cook*
High Wycombe, *R Goodearl*
Around Stony Stratford, *A Lambert*

CHESHIRE

Cheshire Railways, *M Hitches*
Chester, *S Nichols*

CLWYD

Clwyd Railways, *M Hitches*

CLYDESDALE

Clydesdale, *Lesmahagow Parish Historical Association*

CORNWALL

Cornish Coast, *T Bowden*
Falmouth, *P Gilson*
Lower Fal, *P Gilson*
Around Padstow, *M McCarthy*
Around Penzance, *J Holmes*
Penzance and Newlyn, *J Holmes*
Around Truro, *A Lyne*
Upper Fal, *P Gilson*

CUMBERLAND

Cockermouth and District, *J Bernard Bradbury*
Keswick and the Central Lakes, *J Marsh*
Around Penrith, *F Boyd*
Around Whitehaven, *H Fancy*

DERBYSHIRE

Derby, *D Buxton*
Around Matlock, *D Barton*

DEVON

Colyton and Seaton, *T Gosling*
Dawlish and Teignmouth, *G Gosling*
Devon Aerodromes, *K Saunders*
Exeter, *P Thomas*
Exmouth and Budleigh Salterton, *T Gosling*
From Haldon to Mid-Dartmoor, *T Hall*
Honiton and the Otter Valley, *J Yallop*
Around Kingsbridge, *K Tanner*
Around Seaton and Sidmouth, *T Gosling*
Seaton, Axminster and Lyme Regis, *T Gosling*

DORSET

Around Blandford Forum, *B Cox*
Bournemouth, *M Colman*
Bridport and the Bride Valley, *J Burrell & S Humphries*
Dorchester, *T Gosling*
Around Gillingham, *P Crocker*

DURHAM

Darlington, *G Flynn*
Darlington: A Second Selection, *G Flynn*
Durham People, *M Richardson*
Houghton-le-Spring and Hetton-le-Hole, *K Richardson*
Houghton-le-Spring and Hetton-le-Hole:
  A Second Selection, *K Richardson*
Sunderland, *S Miller & B Bell*
Teesdale, *D Coggins*
Teesdale: A Second Selection, *P Raine*
Weardale, *J Crosby*
Weardale: A Second Selection, *J Crosby*

DYFED

Aberystwyth and North Ceredigion,
  Dyfed Cultural Services Dept
Haverfordwest, *Dyfed Cultural Services Dept*
Upper Tywi Valley, *Dyfed Cultural Services Dept*

ESSEX

Around Grays, *B Evans*

GLOUCESTERSHIRE

Along the Avon from Stratford to Tewkesbury, *J Jeremiah*
Cheltenham: A Second Selection, *R Whiting*
Cheltenham at War, *P Gill*
Cirencester, *J Welsford*
Around Cirencester, *E Cuss & P Griffiths*
Forest, The, *D Mullin*
Gloucester, *J Voyce*
Around Gloucester, *A Sutton*
Gloucester: From the Walwin Collection, *J Voyce*
North Cotswolds, *D Viner*
Severn Vale, *A Sutton*
Stonehouse to Painswick, *A Sutton*
Stroud and the Five Valleys, *S Gardiner & L Padin*
Stroud and the Five Valleys: A Second Selection,
  S Gardiner & L Padin
Stroud's Golden Valley, *S Gardiner & L Padin*
Stroudwater and Thames & Severn Canals,
  E Cuss & S Gardiner
Stroudwater and Thames & Severn Canals: A Second
  Selection, *E Cuss & S Gardiner*
Tewkesbury and the Vale of Gloucester, *C Hilton*
Thornbury to Berkeley, *J Hudson*
Uley, Dursley and Cam, *A Sutton*
Wotton-under-Edge to Chipping Sodbury, *A Sutton*

GWYNEDD

Anglesey, *M Hitches*
Gwynedd Railways, *M Hitches*
Around Llandudno, *M Hitches*
Vale of Conwy, *M Hitches*

HAMPSHIRE

Gosport, *J Sadden*
Portsmouth, *P Rogers & D Francis*

HEREFORDSHIRE

Herefordshire, *A Sandford*

HERTFORDSHIRE

Barnet, *I Norrie*
Hitchin, *A Fleck*
St Albans, *S Mullins*
Stevenage, *M Appleton*

ISLE OF MAN

The Tourist Trophy, *B Snelling*

ISLE OF WIGHT

Newport, *D Parr*
Around Ryde, *D Parr*

JERSEY

Jersey: A Third Selection, *R Lemprière*

KENT

Bexley, *M Scott*
Broadstairs and St Peter's, *J Whyman*
Bromley, Keston and Hayes, *M Scott*
Canterbury: A Second Selection, *D Butler*
Chatham and Gillingham, *P MacDougall*
Chatham Dockyard, *P MacDougall*
Deal, *J Broady*
Early Broadstairs and St Peter's, *B Wootton*
East Kent at War, *D Collyer*
Eltham, *J Kennett*
Folkestone: A Second Selection, *A Taylor & E Rooney*
Goudhurst to Tenterden, *A Guilmant*
Gravesend, *R Hiscock*
Around Gravesham, *R Hiscock & D Grierson*
Herne Bay, *J Hawkins*
Lympne Airport, *D Collyer*
Maidstone, *I Hales*
Margate, *R Clements*
RAF Hawkinge, *R Humphreys*
RAF Manston, *RAF Manston History Club*
RAF Manston: A Second Selection,
  RAF Manston History Club
Ramsgate and Thanet Life, *D Perkins*
Romney Marsh, *E Carpenter*
Sandwich, *C Wanostrocht*
Around Tonbridge, *C Bell*
Tunbridge Wells, *M Rowlands & I Beavis*
Tunbridge Wells: A Second Selection,
  M Rowlands & I Beavis
Around Whitstable, *C Court*
Wingham, Adisham and Littlebourne, *M Crane*

LANCASHIRE

Around Barrow-in-Furness, *J Garbutt & J Marsh*
Blackpool, *C Rothwell*
Bury, *J Hudson*
Chorley and District, *J Smith*
Fleetwood, *C Rothwell*
Heywood, *J Hudson*
Around Kirkham, *C Rothwell*
Lancashire North of the Sands, *J Garbutt & J Marsh*
Around Lancaster, *S Ashworth*
Lytham St Anne's, *C Rothwell*
North Fylde, *C Rothwell*
Radcliffe, *J Hudson*
Rossendale, *B Moore & N Dunnachie*

LEICESTERSHIRE

Around Ashby-de-la-Zouch, *K Hillier*
Charnwood Forest, *I Keil, W Humphrey & D Wix*
Leicester, *D Burton*
Leicester: A Second Selection, *D Burton*
Melton Mowbray, *T Hickman*
Around Melton Mowbray, *T Hickman*
River Soar, *D Wix, P Shacklock & I Keil*
Rutland, *T Clough*
Vale of Belvoir, *T Hickman*
Around the Welland Valley, *S Mastoris*

LINCOLNSHIRE

Grimsby, *J Tierney*
Around Grimsby, *J Tierney*
Grimsby Docks, *J Tierney*
Lincoln, *D Cuppleditch*

Scunthorpe, *D Taylor*
Skegness, *W Kime*
Around Skegness, *W Kime*

LONDON

Balham and Tooting, *P Loobey*
Crystal Palace, Penge & Anerley, *M Scott*
Greenwich and Woolwich, *K Clark*
Hackney: A Second Selection, *D Mander*
Lewisham and Deptford, *J Coulter*
Lewisham and Deptford: A Second Selection, *J Coulter*
Streatham, *P Loobey*
Around Whetstone and North Finchley, *J Heathfield*
Woolwich, *B Evans*

MONMOUTHSHIRE

Chepstow and the River Wye, *A Rainsbury*
Monmouth and the River Wye, *Monmouth Museum*

NORFOLK

Great Yarmouth, *M Teun*
Norwich, *M Colman*
Wymondham and Attleborough, *P Yaxley*

NORTHAMPTONSHIRE

Around Stony Stratford, *A Lambert*

NOTTINGHAMSHIRE

Arnold and Bestwood, *M Spick*
Arnold and Bestwood: A Second Selection, *M Spick*
Changing Face of Nottingham, *G Oldfield*
Mansfield, *Old Mansfield Society*
Around Newark, *T Warner*
Nottingham: 1944–1974, *D Whitworth*
Sherwood Forest, *D Ottewell*
Victorian Nottingham, *M Payne*

OXFORDSHIRE

Around Abingdon, *P Horn*
Banburyshire, *M Barnett & S Gosling*
Burford, *A Jewell*
Around Didcot and the Hagbournes, *B Lingham*
Garsington, *M Gunther*
Around Henley-on-Thames, *S Ellis*
Oxford: The University, *J Rhodes*
Thame to Watlington, *N Hood*
Around Wallingford, *D Beasley*
Witney, *T Worley*
Around Witney, *C Mitchell*
Witney District, *T Worley*
Around Woodstock, *J Bond*

POWYS

Brecon, *Brecknock Museum*
Welshpool, *E Bredsdorff*

SHROPSHIRE

Shrewsbury, *D Trumper*
Whitchurch to Market Drayton, *M Morris*

SOMERSET

Bath, *J Hudson*
Bridgwater and the River Parrett, *R Fitzhugh*
Bristol, *D Moorcroft & N Campbell-Sharp*
Changing Face of Keynsham,
  B Lowe & M Whitehead
Chard and Ilminster, *G Gosling & F Huddy*
Crewkerne and the Ham Stone Villages,
  G Gosling & F Huddy
Around Keynsham and Saltford, *B Lowe & T Brown*
Midsomer Norton and Radstock, *C Howell*
Somerton, Ilchester and Langport, *G Gosling & F Huddy*
Taunton, *N Chipchase*
Around Taunton, *N Chipchase*
Wells, *C Howell*
Weston-Super-Mare, *S Poole*
Around Weston-Super-Mare, *S Poole*
West Somerset Villages, *K Houghton & L Thomas*

STAFFORDSHIRE

Aldridge, *J Farrow*
Bilston, *E Rees*
Black Country Transport: Aviation, *A Brew*
Around Burton upon Trent, *G Sowerby & R Farman*
Bushbury, *A Chatwin, M Mills & E Rees*
Around Cannock, *M Mills & S Belcher*
Around Leek, *R Poole*
Lichfield, *H Clayton & K Simmons*
Around Pattingham and Wombourne, *M Griffiths,*
  P Leigh & M Mills
Around Rugeley, *T Randall & J Anslow*
Smethwick, *J Maddison*
Stafford, *J Anslow & T Randall*
Around Stafford, *J Anslow & T Randall*
Stoke-on-Trent, *I Lawley*
Around Tamworth, *R Sulima*
Around Tettenhall and Codsall, *M Mills*
Tipton, Wednesbury and Darlaston, *R Pearson*
Walsall, *D Gilbert & M Lewis*
Wednesbury, *I Bott*
West Bromwich, *R Pearson*

SUFFOLK

Ipswich: A Second Selection, *D Kindred*
Around Ipswich, *D Kindred*
Around Mildenhall, *C Dring*
Southwold to Aldeburgh, *H Phelps*
Around Woodbridge, *H Phelps*

SURREY

Cheam and Belmont, *P Berry*
Croydon, *S Bligh*
Dorking and District, *K Harding*
Around Dorking, *A Jackson*
Around Epsom, *P Berry*
Farnham: A Second Selection, *J Parratt*
Around Haslemere and Hindhead, *T Winter & G Collyer*
Richmond, *Richmond Local History Society*
Sutton, *P Berry*

SUSSEX

Arundel and the Arun Valley, *J Godfrey*
Bishopstone and Seaford, *P Pople & P Berry*
Brighton and Hove, *J Middleton*
Brighton and Hove: A Second Selection, *J Middleton*
Around Crawley, *M Goldsmith*
Hastings, *P Haines*
Hastings: A Second Selection, *P Haines*
Around Haywards Heath, *J Middleton*
Around Heathfield, *A Gillet & B Russell*
Around Heathfield: A Second Selection,
  A Gillet & B Russell
High Weald, *B Harwood*
High Weald: A Second Selection, *B Harwood*
Horsham and District, *T Wales*

Lewes, *J Middleton*
RAF Tangmere, *A Saunders*
Around Rye, *A Dickinson*
Around Worthing, *S White*

WARWICKSHIRE

Along the Avon from Stratford to Tewkesbury, *J Jeremiah*
Bedworth, *J Burton*
Coventry, *D McGrory*
Around Coventry, *D McGrory*
Nuneaton, *S Clews & S Vaughan*
Around Royal Leamington Spa, *J Cameron*
Around Royal Leamington Spa: A Second Selection,
  J Cameron
Around Warwick, *R Booth*

WESTMORLAND

Eden Valley, *J Marsh*
Kendal, *M & P Duff*
South Westmorland Villages, *J Marsh*
Westmorland Lakes, *J Marsh*

WILTSHIRE

Around Amesbury, *P Daniels*
Chippenham and Lacock, *A Wilson & M Wilson*
Around Corsham and Box, *A Wilson & M Wilson*
Around Devizes, *D Buxton*
Around Highworth, *G Tanner*
Around Highworth and Faringdon, *G Tanner*
Around Malmesbury, *A Wilson*
Marlborough: A Second Selection, *P Colman*
Around Melksham,
  Melksham and District Historical Association
Nadder Valley, *R. Sawyer*
Salisbury, *P Saunders*
Salisbury: A Second Selection, *P Daniels*
Salisbury: A Third Selection, *P Daniels*
Around Salisbury, *P Daniels*
Swindon: A Third Selection, *The Swindon Society*
Swindon: A Fourth Selection, *The Swindon Society*
Trowbridge, *M Marshman*
Around Wilton, *P Daniels*
Around Wootton Bassett, Cricklade and Purton, *T Sharp*

WORCESTERSHIRE

Evesham to Bredon, *F Archer*
Around Malvern, *K Smith*
Around Pershore, *M Dowty*
Redditch and the Needle District, *R Saunders*
Redditch: A Second Selection, *R Saunders*
Around Tenbury Wells, *D Green*
Worcester, *M Dowty*
Around Worcester, *R Jones*
Worcester in a Day, *M Dowty*
Worcestershire at Work, *R Jones*

YORKSHIRE

Huddersfield: A Second Selection, *H Wheeler*
Huddersfield: A Third Selection, *H Wheeler*
Leeds Road and Rail, *R Vickers*
Pontefract, *R van Riel*
Scarborough, *D Coggins*
Scarborough's War Years, *R Percy*
Skipton and the Dales, *Friends of the Craven Museum*
Around Skipton-in-Craven, *Friends of the Craven Museum*
Yorkshire Wolds, *I & M Sumner*